Lost in the Bardo

Lost in the Bardo

Poems by

Carolynn Kingyens

© 2026 Carolynn Kingyens. All rights reserved.
This material may not be reproduced in any form, published,
reprinted, recorded, performed, broadcast,
rewritten or redistributed without
the explicit permission of Carolynn Kingyens.
All such actions are strictly prohibited by law.

Cover design by Shay Culligan
Cover image by Luca Bravo on Unsplash
Author photo by Carolynn Kingyens

ISBN: 979-8-90146-703-9

Kelsay Books
502 South 1040 East, A-119
American Fork, Utah 84003
Kelsaybooks.com

For my mother—
a mystery

Acknowledgments

Grateful acknowledgment is made to the publications in which the following poems first appeared:

The Five-Two: “Duper’s Delight”

ONE ART: a journal of poetry: “Atrocities,” “What Has Become of the First Marriage,” “The Mantra of a Teratoma”

Red Eft Review: “Regression at the Middle-Age Soirée,” “Talking to Myself,” “Orbit / Obit,” “Time Bomb,” “Cat’s in the Cradle, “Lost in the Bardo”

The Somerville Times: “Cat’s in the Cradle”

Contents

Their doormat reads:

My Consequences Don't Live Here Anymore,

and for a while, this is true.

—Carolynn Kingyens,
Before the Big Bang Makes a Sound

Cat's in the Cradle

My black, jade-eyed cat
and I press our noses
squarely against the coolness
of the kitchen's window screen
but for totally different reasons:
his, out of infinite pining
for feral-freedom,
hunting mice and birds
with reckless abandon
before his entrapment
and ultimate rescue
for the safe, mundane life
of an indoor cat,
always ready to bolt;
and mine, for relief
from a searing hot flash
while stirring a large pot
of homemade sauce,
where I add a few pinches
of baking soda
to cut into the acidity
of garden-variety tomatoes;
just the two of us,
side by side,
our heads leaning,
almost touching
while we stare out
into the vast, open darkness
of the backyard.

My life has begun to morph
to the mercy of middle age;
to the mercy of teenage daughters
with their scorched earth eye rolls
and ignored text messages
after spamming their phones
with sentimental mother-daughter
reels and memes,
a declaration of my love
despite the obvious thud
from the time in their lives
when I was present
but not fully present
long enough for their validated
resentment of me to seed—
take root, and then flourish
like Mimosa Pudica,
a type of foliage known
to quickly fold inward
and droop whenever touched.

If anything, middle age offers
perspective, however precarious,
like the time I swallowed a fly
while riding a Citi Bike
along the Gowanus Canal
as a result of my mouth-breathing.

Now, I'm learning new terms
like active listening, which,
according to the family therapist,
means being able to hold
the ball while listening
to difficult truths, without reacting;
just holding the ball
as heavy as regret.

Atrocities

Hell, he said,
was not a caliente inferno
for demons and lost souls,
but the act
of being completely alone—
Thoreau-style solitude,
in the wilderness
of our own minds
and past lives;
again and again
we are forced to watch
as if held down
by the hand of God,
our atrocities animated
against loved ones.

I was somewhere
between buzzed
and drunk,
sitting inside his
silver sports car
in our parents' driveway
where we were talking
about hell and damnation
of all things,
not quite sure if I was
making sense.

It felt awkward
to sit next to him,
alone, without the familiar
distractions of our loud,
big family—
he in-between girlfriends
and I at home
for the weekend
without the company
of my husband,
but with the company
of my dog.

The glowing-red ember
of his cigarette
burned on and on
and on.

The Bardo I

A distinct feeling
of dread had draped
over my home
like cloth draped
over a birdcage.

It was that thick,
that palpable.

Regression at the Middle Age Soirée

Old age ain't no place for sissies.
—Bette Davis

You're surprised when
Blythe Monk,
your daughter's
soft-spoken preschool teacher
from years ago,
who always smells
of Chanel No.5,
pulls out a sandwich bag
full of neatly-wrapped joints
from her COACH purse.

For a moment,
you think she's holding
a bag full of Bang Snaps,
those white, twist-tie
wrapper explosives
you once threw
on the ground with glee
when you were a child,
decades ago.

You reach in and take two
Bang Snap-joints;
one for now,
one for later.

And you think—
This is middle-age
regression

while standing
in the midst
of middle school parents
at the soirée,
where chardonnay
and Sangria keep
flowing for hours.

Your thoughts ruminate:

My husband is sleeping
in the guest room; says
it's because of my snoring.

My daughter hates me.

I get side cramps
every time I bend over
to zip-up my favorite,
black suede boots.

I hate my life.

You can feel your defenses
fall as trees do—
loud and disastrous.

Next, you're flirting
with your widower neighbor
with the meticulous lawn—

the retired, tight-lipped
CIA agent, who jogs
every single day
at the crack of dawn,
no matter the weather.

His self-discipline shames
you.

His self-discipline shames
everyone at the party.

You drink Sangria
until your mouth has a
port wine-stain mustache.

You twerk on the widower
with the nice lawn.

You twerk on the soft-spoken
Blythe Monk.

You twerk atop
the breakfast bar
until you fall down—
hard.

Nightswimming

It's the anticipation
you missed most,
those youthful days
when you didn't have
to will your weight thin,
wearing a black and white
polka dot bikini with ease
during hot, humid nights
nightswimming.

And those endless games
of Marco Polo,
when you'd lose
your fifth sense of sight,
depending on echolocation—
the way of the dolphin;
the way of the bat.

How you'd almost forgotten
you required sight
the moment a rush
of chlorinated water
moved rapidly across your
dimple-free thighs.

Next, a slight graze
of a fish-gill foot
against your smooth belly;
someone's pulsating wrist
and that glorious anticipation
of a slippery-wet grasp.

Talking to Myself

> *You have made us for yourself,*
> *and our hearts are restless until it rests in you.*
> —Saint Augustine

A seminary student,
whom I once knew
back in college,
an old friend,
who'd lose his faith entirely
after one of the little girls
at a makeshift church
he helped pastor for a time
in Mawlynnong,
the one with the glass eye
the color of jade,
and the cutest giggle,
was raped and strangled
by a group of barefoot
village boys, who'd
plead guilty, then
disappear in the night,
one by one.

Where was God
for that little girl?
he asked me over bottles
of Stella Artois and falafel
after reconnecting on Facebook
after a decade of ghosting.

An atheist now,
and an insomniac,

who'd get high every night
to Coltrane records
and warm baths,
a routine, he said,
that coaxed him to sleep
—just fine.

He told me that he didn't mind
when the glasses clinked loudly
inside the kitchen cupboard
every time the silver bullet
subway train roared
underneath his first floor
apartment in Clinton Hill,
that the sound reminded
him of a cousin's wedding,
where all the guests raised
their goblet glasses high
and clinked them with whatever
silverware was left on their tables:
knives, salad forks, teaspoons,
all in unison,
prodding the groom to kiss
his bride, on demand.

He smiled.

Next, he told me about
Joey Cabrio, the kind,
homeless man he befriended
outside his apartment.

He told me about their
conversations around
the philosophy
of Saint Augustine,
and their shared love
for Coltrane, Lester Young,
and Johnny Hodges,
who'd end up stabbed
to death by another homeless
person off his meds
over some stupid, imaginary
turf war.

Why are humans so evil?
he asked me, now buzzed.

I wanted to say my canned
Christian response to pretty
much all of life's troubles,
the only one I knew—
Because of sin,
Because of free will,

but chose to stay silent
instead.

He told me every time
I prayed to my
Judeo-Christian God
that I was merely
talking to myself.

Do you enjoy talking
to yourself? He quipped
with a fox-like grin.

When I was ten years old,
I came to a quick realization,
on my own,
that for all those years,
all those Saturday afternoons
at my best friend's house
playing Barbies in her basement—
with her Barbie Dreamhouse,
with her Barbie Camper,
with her Barbie McDonald's,
Jen owned all the good toys;
acting out brutal, betraying
scenarios to put our Barbies through:
the cheating scandals
with Ken;

the heartbreak
of the blonde Barbie
with the bad haircut;
the runaway Skipper;
the terminal illness
of Jazzercise Barbie,
that all along I was playing
a little, merciless god,
myself.

And it was at that moment
I was done with Barbies—
for good, moving on
to the pretty, Roman Catholic
boys of St. Anselm's Parish;
once French kissing an altar boy,
resembling Ralph Macchio
from *The Karate Kid*
during an innocuous, pubescent
closet-game of *Seven Minutes*
in Heaven at Jen's thirteenth
birthday party, down in her
basement, where I used to
talk to myself
for hours.

Famished

"Who's your inner-child, Antonia?" Dr. Weiss asked in his calm, grandfatherly voice, almost leaning into the dead air that stood between himself, and his long-standing patient.

A dark-haired woman, whom one could glean by the mathematical ratios of her face, the symmetrical balance of her features, that she was once stunningly beautiful in her prime.

Although still pretty, she now had a vacant look to her doe-shaped eyes. Her mannerisms, the way she carried herself, were a little odd. She walked slower, talked slower, and often felt detached from her everyday life, the reason why she started coming to Dr. Weiss five years ago.

The silence lingered after the question for an abnormally long time. But Dr. Weiss, knowing his patient so well, waited unperturbed. Finally, the quiet, dark-haired woman answered his question:

"My inner child has the appetite of a bear. She's always starving."

The kind doctor sat forward in his chair, completely committed and engaged, almost cutting into that awkward, invisible distance that seemed to surround his patient from all sides, when he asked:

"What is she starving for, Antonia?"

This time, there was no pause after his question.

"I don't think it's about food, Dr. Weiss. I think there are answers only my inner child knows, and every time she wants to come clean, and tell me, I shut her up with food until I feel all numb and warm inside like how I imagine a junkie would feel after a heroin fix."

Antonia, although quirky, was one of Dr. Weiss' favorite patients because of the raw honesty in which she spoke.

"What does your inner child want to tell you?"

Antonia looked down before looking back up again, meeting Dr. Weiss' grayish-blue eyes.

"I don't think my inner child was mirrored normally. So when she was sad that wasn't mirrored back. She was told, instead, to *Get over it,* that she was *Too sensitive,* her feelings were invalidated. So, when she grew up, finally an adult, she could no longer trust her own account of reality, becoming anchorless. She was devalued and disrespected until she believed all the mirrored feedback as truth."

"And what is that truth?" asked Dr. Weiss.

"That I don't matter."

And with those four final words, Antonia began to sob.

From Scratch

For Alma

I didn't know how to bake
from scratch
using egg, oil, flour,
a hint of vanilla.

I didn't know
how to construct a crust
to hold the sweet inside:
spiced apples, ripened peaches;
to hold the savory inside:
minced meat, scrambled eggs,
sharp cheddar.

Recipes are endless
when baking with pie shells,
his mother reminded,
encouraging me to try
as she went to work
in my designer kitchen
rolling endless strips
of pastry dough
atop cold, whitish-gray
marble.

She'd knead nooks
in dough
malleable as an infant,
molded niches with her long,
nimble farm fingers—
an edible, delectable womb,
a crust to hold the love inside
for her only child—a son,
my husband,
who'd request his favorite pie,
strawberry rhubarb,
a recipe passed down
from her mother's mother
to be lost
on her son's wife.

The Bardo II

We learned young
religion was thicker
than blood,
blood thicker
than San Pellegrino.

Duper's Delight

A liar tells me
there is no such
thing as truth,
that truth is as fluid
as sex.

The liar says
This is my truth
and everyone
believes her.

The liar says
I am the victim here
and no questions
are asked.

The problem,
she says,
is my perception
as if truth is something
we could trap
under a glass
the way we trap light beams
and insects.

Lies, she says,
travel faster
than the speed
of light.

She says *the truth*

has many sides
like a shiny diamond
on the finger
of a Las Vegas
blackjack dealer.

She says *the truth*
has many sides
like a colossal glacier
in the middle of
Antarctica.

She says *truth*
is a shit show,
a dumpster fire
in a tin roof trailer park
some twenty miles
from the nearest highway
in flood-prone Florida.

Truth is ugly,
the fat friend,
the sidekick
who never gets laid.

Lying, she says,
is a luxury
I can never afford.

Fever Dream

I will write about it,
but not today, not now,
not when the lump
in my throat
is a permanent buoy—
the pit in my stomach
that broke away,
a free radical
filled with rage:
Look at what loving you
has cost me!
I scream in my dreams
to no one.

In my dreams,
I have no voice.
In my dreams,
I have no voice,
and I'm in a room
full of familiar faces.

In my dreams,
I have no voice,
and I'm in a room
full of familiar faces,
and they are celebrating
someone's birthday.

In my dreams,
I have no voice,

and I’m in a room
full of familiar faces,
and they are celebrating
someone’s birthday,
but they pretend
I’m not there,
or they can’t see me—
I never quite know for sure,
either way.

I hug myself to sleep,
whatever sleep is,
whatever this is—
half-ghost,
far from whole.

The Bardo III

When I asked my brother
how he lived
with all the elephants
in the room, he'd respond
in a rather matter-of-fact tone
as if the answer was universally
obvious to everyone,
but me:

I carry peanuts
in my pockets.

Googling Sharon Olds' Ex-Husband After Reading *Stag's Leap*

Talk sweetly to yourself.
Take care of yourself.
—Sharon Olds

I must admit
it felt a bit invasive,
a bit stalkerish
to Google the ex-husband
of Sharon Olds,
trying to put a face
to the heartbreak
after reading her award-winning
book *Stag's Leap*;
a man whom she'd never
publicly named,
or shamed, as a once—
scorned wife,
if not for his sake,
then for the sake
of their two adult children,
who are probably my age,
by now.

Reading *Stag's Leap,*
a book detailing the private fallout
from her 32-year marriage
with the quiet restraint
of a poetic saint
rather than a *Bonfire of the Vanities:*
no burning of bespoke suits
and Rolex watches,

jammed inside his luxury, foreign car
parked in front of their pretty house
in full view of the neighbors
like Angela Bassett's Bernadine
in *Waiting to Exhale*;
lighting up a cigarette
right before the epic cinematic torching
of all torching.

No clinginess.

No torrent of texts
at 5am.

No drunken threats
in the middle of the night—
the ongoing histrionics.

No radical haircut
to get her groove back,
sticking, instead,
to her signature style;
those long, loose cords
of white and silver,

comparing her wild mane
to a hairy “shawl,”
calling it her “protection.”

Now, when I squint
my eyes at just the right
angle, I may mistake Sharon
Olds for Patti Smith,
or Natalie Merchant.

The first poetry book
I ever read was *The Dead
and the Living.*

Sharon Olds, the patron saint
of poetry; the patron saint
of how not to lose yourself
when the man you loved
for 32 years comes home
and randomly says,
“I think I’m done”
while in the middle of doing
something unfeeling and routine
like taking off his dress socks
as he rests on the edge
of the bed;
confessing he now sees you,
now loves you
as the mother of his children—
nothing more than that.

Momentary Daydream

You throw plates
against the kitchen floor
the way the Greeks do
while dancing the can-can
barefoot
around the broken
porcelain chips,
lifting your long,
gypsy skirt thigh-high
as your bra strap slopes
down your shoulder
on its own.

You fling your hair clip
clear across the room,
hitting a family portrait
hanging on the wall;
hair collapses
into loose curls
way down your back,
barely touching
your hips.

You let him pick you up
while you wrap your lean legs
around his torso
as he wipes the tabletop
clean behind your back
with one fell swoop
of his fierce tattooed arm;

bills and bananas,
a sleeping cat
and saltshaker
come crashing
to the floor.

You're startled
out of this daydream
when the mute man
sitting beside you asks
for the saltshaker
forgetting for a moment
this is your life,
this is your man
who enjoys his meals
with his head down,
uncommunicative;
the only voices talking
are coming from the radio
atop the refrigerator,
a program dedicated
to conservative commentary.

You go back
to adjusting your bra strap
within the borders
of your tank top
as you glance down
at your purring tabby
sound asleep
against your ankle.

You eat your bowl
of hot chili in silence
while reminiscing
the momentary daydream,
blowing breath
on each steaming spoonful
before swallowing.

Yoko Ono

Megan and Nicolai were in the same Comparative Literature class. He sat two rows behind her. He wore a shirt and tie to class every day, and his hair would appear wet-looking from whatever hair styling product he was overusing. Megan thought he looked like a Mormon missionary with his array of short sleeved shirts and skinny neckties.

The other students, in contrast, looked like they'd gotten dressed in the dark—mismatched socks, shirts inside out, hoodies that hadn't been washed in weeks. Some of the girls, like Megan, preferred to wear their hair in messy top-buns that resembled abandoned nests.

But Nicolai was different. He stood out from the crowd. He caught Megan's eye early in the semester after she'd overheard him speaking to their professor. Nicolai had an accent, but she couldn't yet place it. She'd initially thought Russian, then Romanian.

Nicolai was a mystery to Megan. And she was always a sucker for a good mystery and accent. Her previous boyfriend was from Boston and played defense for their university's hockey team. She adored his accent as well, and thought it cute how he had no filter:

Look at that Chowdahead, not using his blinkah.

Hey Meg, where's the clickah?

Your sistah is wicked-hot.

That no filter-thing would end up proving a problem for Megan after all. She went from thinking it was "cute" to "crazy." Unable to withstand another day, Megan quickly ended things with the Boston hockey player right before an important game, and the team subsequently lost, disqualifying them for the semi-finals. The entire hockey team, including the coach, would go on to blame her for their losing the game. She became the convenient scapegoat.

As a result, Megan's reputation around campus had gone from "cool chic" to "Yoko Ono" overnight. No guy would glance her way, let alone ask her out on a date. It was like she had a sudden case of bad juju.

One morning, Nicolai dropped a piece of crumpled up paper right at Megan's feet as he walked to his seat. She reached her hand down to pick up the small paper-snowball before she turned her head in his direction.

"O-P-E-N," he mouthed to Megan.

She nodded, then gave him a half-smile, not sure of the note's contents.

Megan slowly read what Nicolai had written:

At least I had that, one guy understood me.
—Yoko Ono

The Bardo IV

So next I did
what anyone would do
in that moment—
turned to Google
instead of God.

Orbit / Obit

I would type orbit
instead of obit
right after your pretty name,
which meant *Messenger of God,*
and the middle name
of my eldest,
in the Google search engine
and thought to myself
how fitting the typo—*orbit*
since the majority
of my life would be
spent orbiting around
you and your steady stream
of stories, where I'd like
to cast myself
as your protector
and confronter
of demons;
the strong one,
and an absolute fool.

It was my therapist
who said it had a name,
this thing we shared,
our once closeness—
enmeshment,
the blurred point
where you ended,
and I began.

Think of us

as a patchwork quilt,
or a paper doll chain
holding hands
for all eternity;
smooth edges
blurred and frayed
at random.

A few months ago,
I watched a Netflix
movie, a true story,
about twin sisters
from England
named June and Jennifer,
who did not speak,
developing a language
only they could
understand, becoming
enmeshed, too.

It would be Jennifer
to die first from
acute myocarditis,
a sudden inflammation
of the heart.

And when I went
no contact a decade ago,
I'd think about you every
single day as I wrote
poetry to ghosts,
and ate until I felt
all numb inside.

After I received the call,
I'd scream *Mommy!*
Mommy! Mommy!
as a forty-nine-year-old orphan,
rocking myself into oblivion
atop an unmade bed
in a fancy boutique hotel
in Toronto.

My cries muffled
by the sound
of someone vacuuming
right outside my door.

Time Bomb

Sometimes complicated emotions,
too heavy to bear, require suspension,
not in a mid-air dangling kind of way
like ribboned mistletoe suspended
over a lone threshold,
or a golf course green-colored piñata
in the shape of an angry T-Rex
suspended over the heads
of small children at the birthday party
but rather a suspension
of reality—some faraway,
metaphysical place
Where The Wild Things Are,
and the emotional baggage
I refuse to feel right now;
you know—painful things
like my estranged mother's suicide,
whom I loved from afar,
where it felt safe,
and a nagging dread that history
may repeat itself
as only dysfunction can
so I hit an invisible pause button
on life: on CPAP machines
and separate bedrooms;
on a daughter, whom I can't reach
no matter how hard I try;
on our mid-century modern home
where the floors are made
entirely of delicate eggshells.

But in this suspension,
this pause,
I'm free to binge-watch YouTube
videos under cute animal
channel names like *GeoBeats*
and *Cuddle Buddies,*
becoming a much-needed comfort
in the tumult
like the one about
a lonely black and white yak
named Marge
and a lonely black and white cow
named Maxine
that soon become fast friends
under the swath
of a bright pink and orange sky,
living out the rest of their days
together on a humane ranch
in the middle of Montana.

Or the video about the quirky,
purple-haired retiree
named Pauline,
who rescues a baby squirrel,
she names Ernest
that falls from its nest,
landing serendipitously
in the sanctuary of her backyard.

Pauline ends up remodeling
half her home to accommodate
the on-going gymnastics
of an indoor pet squirrel;
perhaps filling some kind
of maternal void.

It's amazing what I can keep
at bay while suspended
in this jelly-like grief.

For one, an ocean of emotion
resides just outside myself
wanting full entry
the way water demands—
by way of a slow, steady
seep into the depths
of my cracked psyche-boat
as I stay afloat—for now
with the help of non-stop
amusement and Starbucks.

Yesterday, my daughter
called me *Karen,* and right now
there's a massive beehive
suspended under my roof's eave
in the shape of a furious
ticking time bomb
about to fall and scatter,
changing everything—
for good.

The Bardo V

The stigma soon stung
in Northeast Philadelphia,
where I grew up playing Barbie's
with Irish-Catholic school girls;
attending their Holy Communions
in bland, Baptist dresses,
envying the way
their poofy-white dresses twirled—
AND OH HOW THEY'D TWIRL,
those prepubescent-little brides
of Christ.

I was never truly trusted
by their mothers.

What Has Become of the First Marriage

Whenever I see a mature-looking couple,
between early-to-mid sixties,
walking hand-in-hand with that obnoxious
look of late, middle age love,
I immediately know, stronger
than suspicion, that this is a second marriage,
possibly, a third.

Their bodies, still spry,
with the exception of their backs
now weary and slightly leaning
into the semblance
of a *cursive C.*

It's at the garish, fluorescent-lit diner,
known for their early bird specials,
where I spot them next;
sitting side-by-side in the same
maroon-colored polyurethane-pleather
booth reminding me, for a moment,
of that yellow-tinged photograph
from a history book
back in middle school
of a pioneering couple,
sitting side-by-side as the husband
mans a dust-covered wagon
while his wife holds a long,
double barrel shotgun
across her lap during the era
of the California Gold Rush.

I ponder, wondering why
they just can't sit across
from each other like the rest
of us disgruntled, cynical couples
well-seasoned in realism and romance,
knowing full well the value
of separate booths and bedrooms;
the value of personal space.

Perhaps we can blame it on
raising multiple children
notwithstanding the later care
of elderly parents
before the unexpected crash
and subsequent depletion
of your Roth IRA and 401K,
and our failure to launch,
rage-filled man-child, who'd turn us
prematurely gray in our thirties,
and who still keeps us
up at night with endless worry.

This is the kind of tumult
that depletes and desolates
first marriages into abysmal
shreds.

It's as if some imaginary, sci-fi
vortex has sucked every
ounce of lust and desire

clean from the depths
of our loins, leaving our love
cagey and bone-dry.

Now, when you reach out
your retired, manicured
hand across the tabletop;
across the universe;
it feels oddly foreign
and cold as a dead fish
with that thousand-yard
glaucoma-cloudy gaze,
finally yielding to its fate.

The Mantra of a Teratoma

> *Emptiness and boredom:*
> *What a complete understatement.*
> *What I felt was complete desolation.*
> *Desolation, despair and boredom.*
> —Susanna Kaysen, *Girl, Interrupted*

I knew a woman once
who had absorbed
her embryonic, parasitic twin
while in utero
only to show up decades later
masquerading as a brain tumor
on a brain scan
before revealing its true
albeit grotesque identity
to a gaggle of neurosurgeons
who'd gathered round
her open, egg-like skull
as they peered down
in total awe
at this little, shiny ball
of fetal flesh
covered in random sprouts
of human hair, teeth,
and bone.

They call this thing,
this medical monstrosity,
a *teratoma*
some mystical malady
ending in the scary suffix—"oma,"
joining the ranks
among the other omas:
melanoma, lymphoma, glaucoma,

sarcoma, carcinoma—*oma*
meaning abnormal growths.

Those of us who are
either too damaged
by life, by love,
or the lack thereof
morph into relational
"omas" of our own;
these walking,
human-husk monsters
eating the essence
of twin flames,
filling the internal,
howling void.

A Gen-Z philosopher
on YouTube
points to the power
of detachment—
the way of the stoic,
and every morning
I stare at the stranger
in the mirror
reciting a mantra
like some childish game
of *Bloody Mary:*

Observe, don't absorb.

Master the pause.

Starve the drama.

Lost in the Bardo

Two years ago,
the phone call arrived
tragic as a gut-punch,
you know—*That Call . . .*
that call every estranged
adult-child dreads;
one I could never prepare for
even after being asked
by a Manhattan therapist,
the same therapist
who'd inform me that
my sleeping
inside of a sleeping bag
atop the celery-green
shag carpet floor
in my parents' bedroom
curled up next to my mother's
bedside like a loyal labrador
was actually something
called enmeshment,
strange behavior that
could be named.

For seven years,
my father would treat me
like a perpetually
annoying cockblock,
perhaps my mother's goal
all along.

Will you go to her funeral?
he'd ask me in one of our sessions.

My lack of an immediate answer
would later morph
into a hypothetical poem,
a poem about going home
after the dreaded, hypothetical
phone call from the brother,
whom I hadn't seen
in well over a decade,
not because of a lack of love
but rather due to the cringey,
social awkwardness
that existed in all our familial
relationships.

In this hypothetical poem,
I would portray myself
as a total stoic;
didn't cry,
didn't scream
before taking the last
poetic flight
out of LaGuardia.

And when the imaginary plane
circled the Hudson—
the perfect trajectory
to study the river
also embodied with secrets,
I'd sit and stare
out the oval window
looking down at the watery graves
of those poor souls
dismembered and discarded
like Angel Melendez,
the New York City Club-Kid;
murdered and dumped
in the Hudson by Michael Alig,
who'd later be played
by Macaulay Culkin
in *Party Monster.*

I digress.

The first boyfriend
I ever brought home
told me my father's eyes
looked dead
in all his photographs.

In 1997,
I read a short story
by Will Self
called "The End
of the Relationship,"
the last story
from his book *Grey Area,*
about an "emotional
Typhoid Mary"
who'd make
all her lovers' eyes
go dead
just like my father's.

Maybe that was who
my mother was,
maybe that's who
I am by extension of her—
an *emotional Typhoid Mary*;
a F'd up folie à deux,
a loyal labrador
lost in the bardo.

The Bardo VI

I would always be
that sad girl
forever searching
for my father's love
in someone else's eyes—
dilated and high
in the backseat
of smoky Saabs
mouthing lyrics
to favorite songs
no longer on the radio.

If lost in the bardo:

Be still, and know that I am God.
—Psalms 46:10

About the Author

Carolynn Kingyens was born and raised in Northeast Philadelphia, where her red brick row house was prone to chronic leaks. She is the author of the poetry collections, *Before the Big Bang Makes a Sound* (2020) and *Coupling* (2021), both published by Kelsay Books.

Ed Meek, poet, writer, and book reviewer for *The Arts Fuse,* writes: *Kingyens is particularly good at dramatizing paradoxes we cling to in everyday life. She suggests we live lives filled with tragicomedy.*

And Barnes & Noble writes on Instagram: *Contemporary, urban, and impassioned, Carolynn Kingyens' poetry resonates with a darkening echo still felt long after the first read.*

In addition to poetry, Kingyens writes essays, reviews, and short fiction. Two stories were selected for *Best of Fiction,* 2021 and 2023 by *Across the Margin,* a Brooklyn arts & culture webzine. Her short story, "The Invitation," is available at *ATM Storytellers,* a podcast found on Apple Podcasts, Spotify, and Simplecast.

Today, Carolynn lives with her family, including four pets, in Canada.

www.ingramcontent.com/pod-product-compliance
Lightning Source LLC
LaVergne TN
LVHW010543100826
845148LV00013B/2578